IMAGINE WHAT'S POSSIBLE

IMAGINE WHAT'S POSSIBLE

Use the power of your mind to take control of your life during cancer

Jarrod Skole and Gary Skole

American Cancer Society®

Published by the American Cancer Society
Health Promotions
250 Williams Street NW
Atlanta, Georgia 30303 USA

5 4 3 2 1   11 12 13 14 15

Library of Congress Cataloging-in-Publication Data
Skole, Jarrod.
Imagine what's possible : use the power of your mind to take control of your life during cancer / Jarrod Skole and Gary Skole.
p. cm.
ISBN-13: 978-1-60443-037-0 (hardcover : alk. paper)
ISBN-10: 1-60443-037-0 (hardcover : alk. paper)
1. Cancer in children—Patients—Psychology. 2. Cancer in children—Treatment—Psychological aspects. 3. Visualization. I. Skole, Gary M. II. Title.
RC281.C4S54 2011
618.92'994—dc22

2011005541

AMERICAN CANCER SOCIETY
Managing Director, Content: *Chuck Westbrook*
Director, Cancer Information: *Terri Ades, DNP, FNP-BC, AOCN*
Director, Book Publishing: *Len Boswell*
Managing Editor, Books: *Rebecca Teaff, MA*
Books Editor: *Jill Russell*
Book Publishing Coordinator: *Vanika Jordan, MSPub*
Editorial Assistant: *Amy Rovere*

Manufactured by Dickinson Press Inc.
Manufactured in Grand Rapids, MI in March 2011
Job #3861500

Printed in the United States of America
Design and composition by **Carla Mattioli Design & Production, Bel Air, MD**

For more information about cancer, contact your American Cancer Society at **800-227-2345** or **cancer.org.**

For permission to reprint any materials from this publication, contact the publisher at **permissionrequest@cancer.org.**

Quantity discounts on bulk purchases of this book are available. For information, please contact the American Cancer Society, Health Promotions Publishing, 250 Williams Street NW, Atlanta, GA 30303-1002, or send an e-mail to **trade.sales@cancer.org.**

CONTENTS

Imagine Getting Rid of Stress, Fear, and Anxiety

Imagine Not Worrying About IVs, Shots, and Needles

Imagine Yourself Defeating Cancer

Imagine Your Blood Cell Counts Improving

Imagine Your Attitude Is Strong and Positive

SPECIAL THANKS TO—

Carla Mattioli
Joan Rolsky, LCSW
Jacki Skole
Lauren Skole
Ruth Skole, EdD
Terry Skole

INTRODUCTION

MY NAME IS JARROD SKOLE.
I go to school, play soccer and lacrosse, and hang out with my friends. But for a while I couldn't do all these things. That's because when I was ten years old, out of nowhere, I found out that I had cancer, and my life changed overnight.

Things were pretty tough at first. I was suddenly spending a lot of time at the hospital getting tons of tests, having so many surgeries I almost lost count, and getting those really difficult chemotherapy treatments. I had to take shots every night so my blood cell counts would stay up. Still, they kept dipping too low, and I started needing blood transfusions.

After a few months of this craziness, I learned a technique that I think really helped me. It is called imagery, also known as visualization. It was really easy to learn and a lot of fun to do. Best of all, it made me feel really good and more in control of what was happening in my life. Now I want to pass this on to you and other kids with cancer.

Doing visualization is kind of like dreaming, but you are awake. All you do is think about what you want to happen and then have fun imagining it. It can be like your favorite cartoon or video game taking place inside your body. The key is that you need to picture it really happening and see it clearly in your mind.

As it turns out, I am not the only one who uses visualization. Tons of famous athletes, including those on the U.S. Olympic gymnastics team, believe in visualization. World-class cyclists, professional football players, and ballet dancers also use visualization. The good news is that kids and teens are much better at it because we have better imaginations.

This book is filled with colorful images that have been used by me and other kids to help us feel better and take control of our bodies during cancer treatment. I hope these pictures will give you some ideas for doing your own visualization. You can use these images or you can make up your own. You may want your parents to help you a little bit at first, but make sure whatever images you think about are the ones you choose.

Just remember this. Visualization does not always work right away, and there are times when it may not seem to be working at all. That does not mean you should stop trying. After each chemotherapy treatment, no matter how hard I tried, I could not stop feeling sick and throwing up. Although visualization did not help with this side effect, it did help me with a lot of other things.

Now that I am better, I still use visualization when I go for tests, play sports, and do other things in my life. It is a great tool you can always have with you. I hope you enjoy doing it and that it helps you as much as it helped me.

Jarrod

HOW TO DO VISUALIZATION

Performing visualization is very easy. Here are some techniques you can follow. It is important to always remember there is no wrong way to do visualization.

1 Find a place that is quiet. You can visualize while lying in bed, sitting in a quiet room, even while sitting in the car when an adult is driving. Take some deep, even breaths. Breathe in through your nose and out through your mouth (see page 1). This will help you relax.

2 Get a very clear image in your mind. This is really important. Make sure there is a lot of detail. See the colors clearly in your mind. Hear the noises, voices, and music. Feel whatever is going on inside your body. The images can be cartoon-like or realistic.

3 Practice regularly. Two or three times a day is ideal. You only need a few minutes each time, so fitting it in should be easy.

4 Don't expect to suddenly feel different, although you may feel more relaxed, more energized, or simply more confident.

5 Enjoy doing the visualization. You can either use the images in this book or make up your own.

FOR PARENTS

This book is intended to help children learn to use the power of visualization to aid them in their battle with cancer. By teaching them this therapeutic technique, you are helping them feel empowered at a time when things can be very scary. During cancer treatment, the whole world seems to be telling them what to do. They are being given so many strange tests and taking so many medications that their world seems totally out of control. Practicing visualization allows children to feel that they have some control over what is happening to them. It gives them permission to fight on their terms and to be an active participant in this fight, not just a bystander.

Visualization is often much more successful with children than adults because their minds are so open, imaginative, and impressionable. Because of this, the influence a parent or loved one can have is critical. While you may be scared, you must help your child to be positive and strong. Encourage your child to practice the visualizations and be supportive. If you are enthusiastic about doing this, your child will be, too. Younger children may need to have instructions read to them and explained. Older children may prefer to do most of the work by themselves, coming up with their own creative images. Simply encouraging them and being supportive will be a big help.

Sometimes children will try to achieve results that do not happen quickly, or at all. At this point, you may need to explain that the images they are working on take time — that they need to have faith and keep trying. If the results they are hoping for never come, they will need you to help them understand and cope.

This book gives you a tool to help you help your child feel empowered and positive. It is just one tool in your arsenal of weapons. The strength of the mind can be powerful. Best of all, it is free and available to everyone.

BLOWING BUBBLES

Imagine the stress blowing right out of your body.

Taking deep, relaxing breaths is a great way to reduce the stress and fears that can build up inside of you. All you need to do is take in a deep breath through your nose. Let the air fill up inside your belly, then blow it out in a slow, steady stream through your mouth.

Pretend you are blowing bubbles. Try and make each bubble the exact same size as the one before. If you blow too hard, the bubbles will be very big at first and then get very small. If you blow in a slow, steady manner, all the bubbles should be close to the same size.

A great way to learn how to blow bubbles is by using real ones. Take a bottle of liquid soap and a bubble wand and practice taking a deep breath in through your nose, letting the air fill your belly. Then blow out through your mouth into the wand, trying to make all of the bubbles about the same size. Once you do this a few times you should be able to do the same thing without the soap and wand, just using your imagination.

WORRIES FLY AWAY

Imagine watching fear, worry, and stress fly away.

When you feel worried, fearful, or upset, try taking your worries out of your mind by placing them in a giant helium balloon. Watch as the balloon clears the trees, then birds, then clouds until it can no longer be seen. As the balloon sails away, your worries go away with it.

Putting your worries somewhere and then watching them disappear can be very helpful during tough times.

SPACE EXPLORATION

Imagine preparing for an MRI, CT scan, or other procedure.

Having an MRI, CT scan, or other procedure can sometimes be scary. You may feel all alone in a big machine that makes funny noises. If you look at it as an adventure instead of a scary procedure, it may help you get through the process. When you are scheduled for any type of test like this, pretend you are going on an adventure. Maybe all of that fancy equipment is your spaceship, taking you on an exciting adventure, or maybe it is a time machine taking you forward or backward in time. It can be anything you want it to be. When you get into the machine, close your eyes, take a few deep breaths, and let your imagination take you anywhere you want to go. You may find that you don't want the test to end.

BLOW AWAY STOMACH PAIN

Imagine your stomachache going away.

You may find that you often get a stomachache. It may happen when you get nervous before your treatment or surgery, or it may happen at night while you are in bed. One of the best things you can do when this happens is to focus on your breathing. Imagine your stomach pain any way you want to. Maybe it is a big knot in your stomach, or maybe it is so full of air or gas it hurts. Now imagine that every time you take a nice easy breath out through your mouth, whatever is causing the pain gets a little bit smaller.

If your belly is full of air, each breath lets out a little bit more air. If your stomach is in knots, each breath loosens the knot just a little bit. It may take a lot of breathing, but as you do so, little by little, the pain goes away. Eventually, the cause of your problem will be so small, you no longer have a stomachache. Make sure you focus on your breathing, not on the pain.

One trick is to count to four as you breathe in and then blow out slowly and easily while counting to five.

Imagination is more
important than knowledge.

— *Albert Einstein*

DISTRACTION

Imagine things other than what you are worried about.

Pain and fear can often be eased through the power of your mind. By focusing on something other than the thing that is bothering you, you may be able to help yourself feel better. If you are worried about an upcoming procedure, such as surgery or a chemotherapy treatment, try thinking about something else. For example, try remembering everything that is in a room of your house — one with lots of stuff in it. Or choose anything that will make you think and concentrate, such as reciting the times tables, counting by threes, or counting backwards. This technique can also be used to help alleviate pain or to help you fall asleep.

MAGIC NUMBING GLOVE

Imagine your hand or arm getting numb.

This magic glove can be put on just before you are about to get a needle stick in your hand or arm. You might want to work with a professional when doing this for the first time. Take the imaginary glove out of the package and slowly put it on your hand. Make sure you take your time and feel each finger squeezing snugly into each space. Continue to pull the glove onto your hand, pushing it up over your wrist until it reaches your elbow and covers the area where you will be getting the needle stick. As you are sliding on the glove, you can feel the skin beginning to get numb and lose feeling. The longer the glove is on, the more your hand and arm get numb until you can barely feel anything.

Another idea similar to this is to imagine you are dipping your hand into a bowl full of a special numbing solution or even into a big pile of deep snow. Picture in your mind how it would feel and then notice how your arm, hand, port area, or any other part of your body slowly becomes numb and loses feeling.

Now you are ready for the needle stick, not worrying about the pain.

If you can dream it, you can do it.

— *Walt Disney*

THE BATTLE

Imagine the good cells in your body doing battle with the cancer cells.

Imagine that there are two armies inside your body. One army is made up of good cells, and the other army is made up of cancer cells. A big battle takes place between the two armies. The good army cells keep on multiplying, while the cancer army gets smaller and smaller with each battle. Eventually, the good cells are so strong that they kill off the much smaller and weaker cancer army.

Picture the battle clearly and see the good army slowly killing off the cancer cells. Feel how good it is as your army wins each battle.

THE VACUUM

Imagine your body cleaning out the bad cancer cells.

Imagine a vacuum cleaner within your body. The vacuum is being driven by good cells that go all over your body looking for the bad cancer cells so they can suck them into the vacuum and out of your body. Feel them going from one part of your body to another, sweeping through every single part, and cleaning out all of the bad cancer cells. See the cancer cells trying to run away in fear, but the powerful suction gets them!

THE BEAM OF LIGHT

Imagine feeling energized or zapping the cancer cells.

Picture a light coming down from above and going directly
into your body. The light could be from the sun, the stars, or
from anywhere. This beam of light enters your body and is
filled with a powerful energy. Maybe it goes directly to your
tumor and zaps it, or maybe it fills your whole body, giving
it an amazing power to be strong and energized. You can
make the light work for you in any way that's right for you. As
the light beam enters your body, see the energy inside your
body and feel the warmth and power that it brings.

DROPPING CELLS OFF A CLIFF

Imagine your body clearing the cancer cells from inside.

Picture yourself gathering the cancer cells from your body and walking to a beautiful place and dropping them off a cliff, never to return. You can see a beautiful sun rising and birds (which symbolize freedom) flying around. You can envision this area any way you like. It may be a beautiful forest with deer and rabbits running around, or it may be a tropical island paradise. At first, you may find lots of cells to collect. But each day you do this, you may find that there are fewer and fewer cancer cells until, eventually, there are no more cells to find.

CHEMOTHERAPY HERO

Imagine the chemotherapy as a powerful hero defeating cancer.

Imagine that each time you get a chemotherapy treatment, you can see the drugs going into your body. The chemo is very powerful and tells the weak cancer cells to "get out!" See the cancer cells shiver with fear as they know they are beaten and must leave.

Chemotherapy to the rescue!

THE DRILL SERGEANT

Imagine your body creating more good blood cells.

Imagine you have three containers inside your body. Each container contains blood cells and is attached to a vein. One has white cells, another has red cells, and the last one has platelets.

Now imagine there is a drill sergeant who is yelling at all the cells to multiply and get bigger and bigger. You can hear him shouting, "Work it! Work it!" As he yells, the cells respond and eventually fill the entire container all the way to the top.

The next time you need to give blood, imagine that when the needle goes into your vein, it will be sucking the blood from the containers, which are full of all of these good blood cells. Your blood cell counts will be very high!

**Blood Cell Counts
Before Visualization**

**Blood Cell Counts
After Visualization**

THE THERMOMETER

Imagine seeing your blood cell counts go up.

Imagine seeing a thermometer inside your body that allows you to monitor your blood cell counts. Picture your body getting more and more good blood cells. As your blood cell counts go up, a thermometer within your body fills up. You can see the blood cell counts starting at a lower level and then rising, eventually bursting through the top of the thermometer.

Imagination rules the world.

— *Napoleon Bonaparte*

THE FACTORY

Imagine producing good blood cells and increasing your energy.

Imagine there is a factory within your body. It can be a toy factory, chocolate factory, or any other type of factory that you imagine. The factory is very busy. There are three chimneys. Instead of smoke coming out, one chimney is producing red blood cells, another white blood cells, and the last one platelets.

The good blood cells fly out of the chimney and pile up within your body. You can feel the energy produced by the factory and all of these new blood cells.

FEEL THE MUSIC

Imagine zapping your cancer cells.

Imagine yourself having any one of your favorite singers inside your body, singing one of your favorite songs. Sing the song to yourself and feel it inside your body. The song will put the cancer cells in a trance, and they will do whatever you want them to do. For example, at the next chemo treatment, the song will make the cancer come out of its hiding spot and get zapped by the chemo.

SUPERHERO

Imagine feeling strong, powerful, and full of energy.

There may be times when you are feeling scared and afraid. That is OK. Cancer can be very scary. Picture yourself as your favorite superhero. Imagine that you are strong, powerful, and full of energy. You know that there is evil out there trying to defeat you, but you are a superhero. You are able to defeat your enemies.

Create the highest, grandest vision possible for your life, because you become what you believe.

— *Oprah Winfrey*

POWER OF LOVE AND TRUST

Allow your family, friends, and medical team to give you extra support.

There are many things that will help you feel better. One of the most important is your positive attitude. Never stop believing that you will get better. Knowing you have the best medical care in the world is very important. You must trust and have faith in your doctors, nurses, social workers, and everyone else who is working so hard to make you better. They are very smart people. Believe in what they are doing.

Believe also in the love you receive from family, friends, and other well-wishers. All of these people are there supporting you. With their love and knowledge, you've got a winning team that can defeat anything. Allow them to help, but never stop believing in you. A positive attitude is a very, very strong weapon.

Promise me you will always remember:
You are braver than you believe, stronger
than you seem, and smarter than you think.

— *Christopher Robin to Pooh*

GLOSSARY

anxiety: fear or feeling worried about something.

benign: not cancer; not malignant.

blood: the fluid in the body that is made up of red blood cells, white blood cells, platelets, and plasma.

blood cell count: a test in which a sample of blood is taken to check for the number of red blood cells, white blood cells, and platelets. Also called a CBC (complete blood count).

blood transfusion: a procedure in which an infusion of blood is given to a person from another person who donated it. In some cases, blood may be taken from a patient earlier and stored until it is needed.

cancer: not just one disease but a group of diseases. All forms of cancer cause cells in the body to change and grow out of control. Most types of cancer cells form a lump or mass called a tumor.

cells: the basic components or "building blocks" that make up tissues in the human body. Cells are found in all living things.

chemotherapy: treatment with drugs to destroy cancer cells. Chemotherapy is often used alone or with surgery or radiation to treat cancer that has spread.

computed tomography (CT): an imaging test in which many x-rays are taken of a part of the body from different angles to produce pictures of the inside of the body. CT scans show much more detail than regular x-rays and help doctors diagnose problems such as cancer. Also called a CAT scan.

diagnosis: the process of identifying a disease by its signs and symptoms and by using imaging tests and laboratory findings.

magnetic resonance imaging (MRI): a safe and painless test that uses a powerful magnet to send radio waves through the body to produce detailed pictures of the body's organs and structures.

malignant: a mass of cells that may invade surrounding tissues or spread to distant areas of the body.

oncologist: a doctor with special training in the diagnosis and treatment of cancer.

pediatric oncologist: a doctor who specializes in treating children with cancer.

plasma: a clear, yellowish part of the blood that carries nutrients, hormones, and proteins throughout the body.

platelets: tiny cells in the blood that help blood clot.

procedure: a test or type of treatment performed by a member of the health care team, designed to obtain information or provide care for the patient.

red blood cells: cells that deliver oxygen to all parts of the body.

surgery: an operation or procedure to remove or repair a part of the body or to find out whether disease is present.

symptom: a change in the body caused by an illness, as described by the person experiencing it.

tissue: a group of cells that have a specific function.

tumor: an abnormal lump or mass of tissue. Tumors can be benign (noncancerous) or malignant (cancerous).

visualization: an activity involving the use of the imagination in order to achieve a desired outcome.

white blood cells: cells that are part of the germ-fighting immune system. White blood cells attack invaders such as viruses and bacteria in order to fight infection.

x-ray: a form of radiation that can be used at low levels to produce an image of the body on film or at high levels to destroy cancer cells.

THE ILLUSTRATORS

We would like to give special thanks to all the illustrators who generously donated their time and talent to produce the wonderful pictures for this book.

Nikolett Nádházi – *The Drill Sergeant, The Factory*

Kathy O'Malley – *Magic Numbing Glove*

Larissa Clause – *Dropping Cells Off a Cliff*

Lauren Skole – *The Thermometer*

Marie Thrasher – *Worries Fly Away, Superhero*

Bridgette McMahon – *Chemotherapy Hero*

Ryan Hoxworth – *Power of Love and Trust*

Afton Metkowski – *The Battle*

Jennifer Hoxworth – *The Vacuum, Feel the Music*

Deborah Flamholz – *Distraction*

Lauren Gulino – *The Beam of Light*

Mike Anderson – *Blow Away Stomach Pain*

Jonathan Swartz – *Blowing Bubbles*

Corinne Mitchell – *Space Exploration*

JARROD SKOLE

 JARROD SKOLE lives in Mt. Laurel, New Jersey. He enjoys playing soccer, lacrosse, and golf, and spending time with family and friends. At the age of ten, Jarrod received a diagnosis of a rare form of bladder cancer. During cancer treatment, he found the mind/body technique called visualization to be extremely helpful. He adapted an adult version of this technique to one better suited for children. Jarrod wrote this book in order to share the simple but powerful concept of visualization with other children going through treatment for illness or other difficult situations.

GARY SKOLE

GARY SKOLE owns and operates businesses that provide in-home care for seniors and disabled adults. He is actively involved in several cancer-related charities and founded the nonprofit organization Imagining Hope with his wife, Terry. This organization is dedicated to helping children with cancer by spreading son Jarrod's message of hope and empowerment. Gary and Terry also have a daughter, Lauren, who contributed artwork to this book.

Other Books for Children from the American Cancer Society

Available everywhere books are sold and online at cancer.org/bookstore

---

Because... Someone I Love Has Cancer

Get Better! Communication Cards for Kids & Adults

Healthy Me: A Read-Along Coloring & Activity Book

I Can Survive

Jacob Has Cancer: His Friends Want to Help (coloring book)

Kids' First Cookbook: Delicious-Nutritious Treats to Make Yourself!

Let My Colors Out

The Long and the Short of It: A Tale About Hair

Mom and the Polka-Dot Boo-Boo

Nana, What's Cancer?

No Thanks, but I'd Love to Dance: Choosing to Live Smoke Free

Our Dad Is Getting Better

Our Mom Has Cancer (available in hardcover and paperback)

Our Mom Is Getting Better

The Survivorship Net: A Parable for the Family, Friends, and Caregivers of People with Cancer

What's Up with Bridget's Mom? Medikidz Explain Breast Cancer

What's Up with Richard? Medikidz Explain Leukemia

Visit cancer.org/bookstore for a full listing of books published by the American Cancer Society.